In Her Own Special Voice

Wendy's ongoing journey with healing and enduring faith

P.S. Ferguson

Praying you will sense God's peace as you read.
Mark 10:27
Pam & Wendy
Feb /16

TABLE OF CONTENTS   Page

Dedications

This work is lovingly dedicated to my two sisters and my boys.

Wendy – Through all these years and through all these times, your life has been more important than you can imagine. You smile through your pain, you laugh in spite of it all, and you are the one person I know who truly embodies the hope of their salvation. When we all get to the other side, you can dance with everyone else, but with Rebecca and me; the three of us are going to sing our hearts out together for Jesus for all eternity.

Rebecca – *"A cord of three strands is not quickly torn apart. Eccl 4:12 (NAS)"* God knew that Wendy and I could not do it on our own. He knew we needed you to be our third strand so none of us would break. You bring the balance, the levity and the meaning to our little cord. You are the glue that ends up holding us all together. Thank you for being exactly everything you are.

Mike and Sam – You are both my treasures. My hope is that you gain just a little more insight into your Aunt Wendy through this work. Family is everything.

And.....

None of it means anything if Jesus is not lifted up.

Thine, O LORD, is the greatness, and the power, and the glory, and the victory, and the majesty: for all that is in the heaven and in the earth is thine; thine is the kingdom, O LORD, and thou art exalted as head above all. 1 Chron. 29:11 KJ

Foreword

Reverend David Mainse
Crossroads Media Group

"Wendy's parents were expecting their second of three children. All of us in their Bethel Church family loved them very much and were excited for their new arrival.

As their pastor, I was particularly filled with joy for them, but also, as always when children are expected, I had deep concern that all would be well for mother and new baby.

That was 46 years ago. My memories are clear.

On a balmy October day, those many years ago, I made my way over to the hospital on Hamilton mountain only four to five blocks away from the church at that time.

I was the first person to see and pray over the little gift they named Wendy. She was a tiny person who was supposed to arrive with the amazing potential all newborn children bring into the world. There were serious complications however. For this little one, all was not well.

As is most often the case in times like these, parents are often bewildered and confused, asking in their hearts, 'Why? How could this have happened?' These parents were no different. Again, as their pastor, what could I have said? Trying to give counsel at such a time would have been inappropriate.
I simply put my arms around them and began to ask God for strength for these parents and their precious baby. That day we prayed Wendy would survive, thrive and live. We prayed that she would realize her full potential, discovering life.

Wendy has done this, as you will read in this most moving story. A life changing experience awaits every reader. I had the privilege of experiencing this story first-hand by knowing Wendy and her family through the years.

Wendy's older sister, Pamela, is an inspiring writer and has done a marvelous and heart-piercing job of Wendy's story. Input came from Wendy herself, as well as from the rest of the family.

Congratulations on this one of a kind book.

Well done, Wendy and Pamela.

David Mainse

Foreword

Reverend Dr. Michael Middlebrook
Lead Pastor,
Bethel Gospel Tabernacle, Hamilton, Ontario

I really enjoyed reading the story of Wendy. It is a moving account of a gracious 46 year old woman of strong Christian faith who has lived a miraculous life in spite of serious life-long physical challenges which are detailed in this brief, insightful and eloquent book.

An added bonus to this book is the section titled Wendy's poems. Two vivid and poignant lines from one poem in particular deeply impressed me: "Treat me like I'm normal...But love me like I'm special." Wow!

I've had the privilege of knowing Wendy for 33 years. She is normal. She's a Canadian and she loves hockey! She is special!

Everybody who knows Wendy will attest that her faith-based life has impacted them in a very special way.

I hope and pray that this biblically balanced, inspirational book gains a wide readership. Those who read this book will be encouraged and edified.

Pastor Mike

PREFACE

This is a work of creative non-fiction.

Wendy is my sister. This is not her biography, nor did this interview actually happen.

The events referred to in the interview did happen, and the details of Wendy's life as written here, also are fact.

The poems were not written by Wendy, however each word of both this story and the poems, have been read carefully to her to make sure she approved of everything written in her name. She made changes where she felt something wasn't right. The poems are written in Wendy's voice to allow some of her thoughts to permeate this powerful story. I would never presume to know what she thinks or how she manages to keep her faith as strong as she does. If she had her own voice to express it, or her own capability to write down her thoughts, she would be far more eloquent than I.

Everything written here is a testament to the life of a woman who deserves honour and respect. It was put together in order to validate her journey, but also to give hope and comfort to those who find themselves at various points along their own path, perhaps similar to Wendy or her parents.

One thing is certain though. Being around Wendy usually brings out the best in people, and those of us fortunate enough to spend any time with her, are the better for it. She points us in the direction of peace, using no words and through a body that does not work.

Miracles abound every day. Not just for Wendy, but for all of us.

What I Know

At the end of the day
This is all I
Truly know

Through all the
Pain and the tears
He is here
Loving me

He gives me
Peace
Love
Joy
In moments
When I need Him

Through all the
Pain and the tears
I am here
Loving Him
With all my broken heart

Sometimes that's all
I really need to know

....Wendy
From 'The Wendy Poems'

CHAPTER ONE

The man watched the older couple enter the hotel lobby. He knew them right away. The woman was pleasant looking, beautiful in the way women are when they age gracefully. The man had a look about him, kind eyes, almost like an older, healthier Elvis if Elvis hadn't abused himself to death.

He had requested them to meet him here for a couple reasons. He wanted the setting to be neutral ground, not much emotion here. People coming and going, lots of movement. They could have a good discussion without any sentimentality here. He also had a plane to catch, which made this place convenient for his leaving later.

When he had contacted them and made arrangements to meet, he had asked them to sit at a table in the hotel restaurant, wait, and he would join them there. He watched them from a distance for a few minutes so he could observe how they interacted, their demeanor, their body language. He could see them chatting between themselves, probably commenting on how the next couple of hours would go. Overall, they seemed like regular people, both had kindness in their smiles and both seemed a bit nervous, perhaps on edge not knowing what to expect.

Walking over to the table, he introduced himself and thanked them for coming. "You must be Wendy's mother? Thank you for coming. Wendy's father? Also sir, thank you for making the time."

Pulling out the chair, the reporter sat opposite the father, which had the mother on his right side. He preferred to watch them both, but as the table was set for four, a chair on each side, this would work fine too.

He could feel them watching him, sizing him up, as he sat down. The graying hair at his temples always seemed to put people at ease.

'Now then, can you give us a little more information on what you're looking for? You're writing an article? About Wendy?' the mother took quick control of the situation and got things started nicely.

'Yes, we'll get to all that in one second. Did you order yet? I'm starved, so I'm going to grab a bite. Please feel free to have lunch; it's the least I can do to thank you for coming.'
The waitress came and took orders for sandwiches and coffees all around.

'Now, to get down to it.' At that, the reporter pulled out his phone and set it on the table. 'I work for Manthis, a national news magazine, my work appearing monthly in print, but mostly I write for what appears online on our website.

Our magazine just completed a large investigative series delving into the pockets of religious outbreaks all over the continent.

There are places where they say 'miracles' are happening throughout the US and Canada. We went and spoke with many who attended those meetings, leadership and decision makers, to follow-up on some of their claims. The series of articles generated quite a bit of interest and response from our readers, both believers in the 'miraculous' and non-believers.'

He could see the two of them shift, ever so slightly, in their seats every time he used his fingers as quotation marks around the word miraculous and miracle. He did it on purpose, just to see how they would respond. It wasn't that he was jaded about spiritual things – he actually had no opinion on them whatsoever, but he wanted a fair assessment of the goings-on and needed people who were balanced in their approach. These were just physical tricks he used to evoke an emotional response. He was satisfied with the initial response this couple gave him. He carried on.

'It was suggested that we do a couple of follow-up articles on the other side of that story. As in…'What Happens to your Faith When you Don't Get a Miracle' kind of thing.'

'I'm sorry, but I don't see how we fit into your story' the father said.

'Right, well, I was told that Wendy is a woman who is deeply committed in her faith, and yet remains confined to a chair. What would be interesting is how you folks balance that out with your faith, and most importantly, if we can get Wendy's perspective on that.'

''Hmmm' Wendy's father said quietly, 'what exactly do you want to know about Wendy? You can actually ask her yourself what you need to know.'

'Yes, well….I tried speaking with her, and ….well, she didn't understand me, and I couldn't really understand her myself, so I thought I would come to you folks to help me answer that question. Are you willing to talk to me? For the article, I mean?'

Both parents looked at each other. It wasn't like they hadn't been here before, answering questions about their daughter. They had – many times, in fact. Their middle daughter Wendy was extraordinary – at least that seemed to be the way most people felt after they had been with her. Wendy was disabled – she had Cerebral Palsy, she was spastic, quadriplegic, athetoid and non-verbal. The doctors had not given her even 24 hours to live when she was born, but here she was 46 years later, defying them all.

'Yes, we will answer your questions' replied her dad in a quiet voice, 'on the condition that you speak with Wendy one more time. We can help you understand her, because she understands everything. She knew exactly what you were saying to her, you were the one who could not understand properly. In her own way, she communicates very well.'

'Yes' Wendy's mom continued, 'you just have to understand the cues. We can go back with you, or staff at the house can also help. They are quite willing and open to that sort of thing.'

'Thank you' the reporter said, acknowledging inside himself that they were probably right. The understanding problem lay with him. When he had approached Wendy, she had looked right through him, appearing to look deep into his eyes, which was unnerving for him. For some reason, she made him nervous, and he prided himself on never getting nervous. He didn't want her inside his head.

'Yes, I would be most grateful if you would go back with me to follow-up with her.'

Sandwiches arrived, along with coffees, for which everyone around the little table was grateful. After the waitress made sure everyone was taken care of, the reporter waved her off, instructing her to keep the coffee pot coming back often.

'Perfect – now. To some questions, shall we?' At that the reporter held up his cell phone and asked 'Okay if I record this?'

CHAPTER TWO

Preliminaries out of the way, the reporter started in straight to the heart of the issue.

'Wendy has been bound to her chair since birth, that's correct?' Fairly innocuous questions came quickly and the parents, who knew this story like their own names, took turns answering details.

The cause? Brain damage at birth. Placenta previa.
No. They didn't expect her to live the first night – seizures, convulsing, etc. There wasn't much in the way of good news.
Yes. Taking her home, we just knew we had to try our best. There was no instruction manual for this. None of the parenting books covered it.

'Let's go back in time a bit shall we? I'd like the readers to have a glimpse into a bit of Wendy's medical history. I don't have many questions about this really – a few general broad strokes, if you can fill in some of those.'

'Certainly.'

Wendy's mother began the narrative, but the reporter could tell that they were used to working these moments together as a team. As details began to be presented, one thought from one side of the table would pave the way for another thought or explanation from the opposite side.

'Well Wendy has had many health issues, as most people like her have. Over the years she has had some major surgeries and a few serious bouts with illness. When you talk about miracles, we have had many close calls with Wendy.

There have been moments – milestones – we can point back to and say clearly that if God's Hand had not touched her, we would have lost her.

Cerebral Palsy is not a deteriorating diagnosis, in and of itself – meaning that the degree of damage to the brain remains the same for someone's lifetime, as opposed to other degenerative challenges like MS or ALS. What Cerebral Palsy, or CP, does hinder, though, is the ability to cope with other issues, such as pneumonia, scoliosis, etc. These challenges present hardships for people like Wendy as her body has to work extra hard to recover from and compensate for them. It's extra tricky when your body historically works against you.'

'True enough' the reporter said, 'That must be frustrating for her.'

Wendy's dad added, 'It's very frustrating for her, but also frustrating for those of us trying to help or bring comfort to a body that won't cooperate.'

The mother continued 'When she was six years old, Wendy had the hamstrings cut in both of her legs, to reduce her leg spasms. She remained in an A-frame cast for six weeks following that.

'Later, in her teens, there were three surgeries to improve her tone and reduce pain. Two were called rhizotomies. It is a neurological procedure that destroys problematic nerve roots in the spinal cord to, again, relieve muscle spasms in her legs. The third was a laminectomy. It's a type of decompression surgery that enlarges your spinal canal to relieve pressure on the spinal cord and nerves.

'These surgeries eventually would prove to provide much needed rest from painful spasms for Wendy's body. Over the years, we have spent quite a bit of time at Toronto Sick Kids Hospital.

'When she was 20 years old, her scoliosis had become so severe, it had twisted her rib cage and reduced her breathing capability. It was decided to insert Harrington rods along her spine to help alleviate this, which meant more back surgery.'

Her dad took over at this point, 'She's struggled with mononucleosis, which nearly took her many years ago. A decade ago, during another surgery, there were issues with her esophagus, which left her unable to eat or drink anything by mouth. That change affected her more than most, as it changed her life forever. It meant that she could no longer eat the foods she loved, and it would be impossible to give her liquids by mouth. It also meant more surgery to insert a GI tube for eating.

'More lately, her back has been giving her no end of trouble, as the scoliosis has been shifting her spine along with the rods. She is in quite a bit of pain every day. At this point, there is no surgery that can help her, or fix her back. The rods that had once been the key to helping her breathe now have become her greatest challenge. They cannot be taken out due to scar tissue, so once again, she must deal with a body that does not want to cooperate and is making it nearly impossible for her to find comfort.

'Understanding of course, all of these situations and challenges had to be understood, investigated and cared for, all trying to communicate with someone who cannot express herself in the traditional sense. Months of pain leading up to discovering what her issue is, and then months of recovery time afterwards.

Even just one of these issues would test most of us, but for Wendy those times just keep coming for her.'

CHAPTER THREE

Everyone seemed to need to catch their breath, both parents sipping coffees, needing a refill, and the reporter trying to process all they had told him so far.

From the sounds of it, Wendy's life had been one hardship after another. As he voiced that thought out loud, the reporter was surprised at the answer he received.

'What? No! One hardship after another? No. That is not how we look at her life, and we don't believe Wendy would look at it that way either. So many good times. So many times where light and joy won over her pain', Wendy's dad seemed almost offended at the thought. 'Yes, she has had hardship, there is absolutely no denying that, but there have been truly beautiful moments as well. Whole volumes of books could be written about those.'

'Well, how about touching on a few of those for me' the man said, interested in how anything could possibly balance out the kind of life this woman seemed to have had.

Wendy's mom started, 'From the very beginning, Wendy was treated like just a regular part of the family, which means that she did as much with us as we could humanly do with her.

From having to perform and learn at school, to having fun at the Fall Fair in our town, she was included. Her father made sure she was on rides at the CNE, and he got her up out of her chair and danced with her at her high school grad.

Every summer she had her own vacation at summer camp, sleeping under the stars, canoeing across the lake. She participated in everything that the other girls did if it was humanly possible; Halloween costumes, up all night Christmas

Eve, her sisters made sure she was teased and joked with just like anyone else. It was important for all of us to know that Wendy was an equal part of the family.'

Wendy's father carried on, 'There were a few highlights that don't just happen to everyone. To celebrate the International Year of the Disabled in 1981, a film crew came in 1980 and captured part of Wendy's history in a movie that won a national award and went to New York to be premiered.

'The crew came to our home, our church, and Wendy's school to record Wendy's life. The film was called 'Breakthrough', showing the amazing breakthrough in communication using Blissymbolics for people like Wendy. It featured two other people like her and the differences being able to communicate made for all of them.

'And as if that weren't enough, we got invited as a family to go to the premiere of that movie, at the United Nations Building in New York City. Well, we didn't have the cash for something like that – flights and hotels for the five of us. Long story short – our little town of Caledonia raised enough money for all five of us to fly to New York. Can you imagine? First time flying for us. We got to experience the United Nations building, the New York Zoo, Barnum and Bailey Circus, and Rueben sandwiches. That trip was unbelievable and when I think back to those days and how that all came about, I can't help but say how God made all those doors open. We prayed, sir, and we believed that God was in control.'

Her mother continued, 'Another thing that has been a huge component in Wendy's life is her independence. Just like anyone else, when they reach a certain age, most people want to be independent of their parents. It's all a natural step in becoming an adult, and Wendy didn't want to miss out on anything.

'As every parent with a child who has a disability knows, there is a type of dread when they start nearing the age of 18. As a challenged child or teenager, there are many excellent programs and helps, but once you cross over to adulthood in the eyes of the government, quite a lot of those helps end. At least it did 30 years ago.

'For someone like Wendy, living in an independent situation is extremely complex because she has no way of calling out, or getting anyone's attention. She needs full-time care, ongoing, all the time.

'Wendy had expressed her desire to move out on her own, as her older sister had done. It was natural. Finding a spot for her was another matter altogether.

'In this way, we believe that doors opened up and a new concept of a 'house with care' was conceived. With two other people who had challenges just like Wendy, and lots of aggressive lobbying by parents and caregivers, a house was established in 1998 that would operate as a home, not an institution, where families could come and be a part of Wendy's life, but where she would be independent as an adult. You have no idea how much work went into all of that, but looking at the bigger picture, Wendy needed her independence, and she got it. She still has it. What her physical care looks like has changed over the 25 years of the homes' existence, and staff come and go, but still, Wendy has had a place of safety to feel that quite normal feeling of living 'on her own' since the beginning.

'And how do the staff treat her?' the man asked. He wondered how these parents, who had invested so much into Wendy, ever managed to let her care be in the hands of others.

'As with anything, there are good reporters and bad reporters,' Wendy's dad said with a smile, 'just like there are good staff and staff who aren't necessarily so great. We all have things like that to deal with in our lives, and so does Wendy.

'She has to accept whoever walks through the door on any given day, in whatever mood they are in, or carrying with them whatever issues they are dealing with at home. Sometimes that makes it challenging to feel secure with caregivers, especially if there are many new people involved, it all tends to get a bit unnerving. Generally, the people who have cared for Wendy have been exceptional. They tend to be above par, usually the cream of the crop, and we couldn't be more pleased.

'Again,' mom continued, 'it must be understood that every part of Wendy's day demands some form of care. She can't move herself from one room to another. She can't shift in her bed if she's uncomfortable in one spot. She can't reposition herself in her chair if she is placed incorrectly. This is where care is so vital.

'For the most part, Wendy has been blessed with caregivers who are kind, compassionate and loving. They have to take care of her most basic needs in a way that still leaves her with her dignity in tact. They speak to her as if she understands them, which she does. We know how her needs are being met because of how she comes to us when we meet her for outings or functions. She is usually happy, confident and looking well put together. If she is having difficulties at home, she works hard to communicate that to us as best she can.

'There haven't always been great staff, and over the years, every once in a while, someone comes along who doesn't quite understand the nature of personal care. When those people come into Wendy's world, you can imagine how frustrating that can be. Again, something that she has no control of in her life, but something she navigates with dignity.'

CHAPTER FOUR

'Perhaps at this point, you can give me a little insight into Wendy's spiritual journey?' the reporter asked.

He had met Wendy and even though he hadn't been able to understand her, and ended up uncomfortable, it still made him feel sorry for her for all the physical troubles she had had to face.

When he was given Wendy's name to be the subject of the follow-up article, he was told she was shining and smiling and always full of light. During their exchange at her home, even though it was frustrating for both of them, she didn't have the hardness or the bitter shell you usually felt in someone who was consumed with their troubles.

By all accounts, this woman had every right to be so full of anger that you should feel her coming a mile away. Nothing could be further from how it felt to be in a room with Wendy. 'She must not feel it, or understand as much as they think she does', he thought to himself, 'otherwise, how would she cope, day after day?'

'Her spiritual journey, certainly.' Again, that tag-team approach to the story-telling took over. Wendy's mom and dad each had a different piece of the story, which would jog the memory of another bit.

Wendy's mother began, 'You need to understand that our home was somewhere God had a place. Faith has always been important to us, and that's how Wendy was raised.

'When Wendy was little, she had a hard time controlling her emotional responses. When she would get overwhelmed inside, she would cry out. What that looked like was crying and loud hollers. We all get overwhelmed at times and need that release, but for Wendy, it was very distracting for people in church services to cope with.

'When she was around seven or eight, at the end of each service, this response kept happening and we did not understand what it meant. Before she was skilled with her symbol board at communicating her feelings, everything with her was a guessing game. Yes and no questions until you hit on the right answer.

'One such night when things were particularly challenging for her, and we were not understanding what she needed, all of the usual questions asked – are you in pain, do you need water, etc, our pastor came and saw that Wendy was in fact crying out to God, wanting to turn control of her heart over to Him.

'In spite of her overwhelmed state, once she made that step of allowing Christ to control her heart, she became peaceful right away because finally someone understood what her heart so desperately needed.

'That was the spiritual awakening we all needed, in regards to Wendy. From that moment on, her heart has been fully given over to her hope and trust and faith in a God who loved her enough to send His Son to die for her.

'Part of our belief system, and subsequently Wendy's, is that we believe that God has a plan for us all. For Wendy, that gives her the knowledge that her life has a meaning and a purpose. God makes no mistakes, nor does He give us anything we cannot handle with Him. As impossible as that sounds, given what she has had to deal with, that is truly what she believes.

'We have never really been alone raising Wendy, and our church family has been important in opening up and accepting Wendy as the beautiful woman that she is.

'Over the years, Pastors have been extremely important in all of that.

'From the very first day of her life, our Pastor at the time came to our hospital room right after we had been given the news about Wendy's condition. It was overwhelming, but in those moments, the Pastor prayed with us over her.

'From her very first moments, her life has been like a Master Class in faith. Pastors and our church family also have accommodated for things like Wendy getting baptized in water, allowing for wheelchairs and accessibility in the building and planning. That might seem to be a common practice now, but over the 46 years of Wendy's life, accommodating the disabled has not always been the priority of decision-makers.

'The praying people, who Wendy trusts with her needs and her hunger for things of God, meet her at every service or Bible study she goes to. She attends church on Sundays, weekly Bible studies and prayer meetings, stays at Family Bible Camp attending camp meetings.

'Her faith is perhaps the strongest thing about her. It is what holds her up and what sustains her through the many impossible times when she feels like giving up.'

CHAPTER FIVE

'Now let's talk miracles' said the reporter, 'clearly Wendy has not experienced hers.'

'Oh, now', Wendy's dad said quickly, 'That's where you are so very wrong. Wendy has had a multitude of miracles, starting with surviving her very first night on earth.'

Wendy's mom leaned forward thoughtfully, 'What strikes me as necessary here is perhaps a bit of clarity on what you mean by miracle. There is no doubt that God has moved and continues to move in the world on the grander scales. There is also no doubting the fact that He is the same yesterday, today and forever, meaning that the same God who healed the lame and the sick in days past is still healing the lame and the sick today.

'Where I think we get a little muddled is our value system. In God's economy, His currency is based on our heart – what's on the inside – the character of a person. It is our natural instinct to place a higher value on what we can see – the larger than life moments. In the end though, everyone must come home from the stadiums and the churches and the hospital rooms and live with grace for the glory of God. It's easier to live in that grace if God heals our attitudes and our hearts, as well as whatever physical issue we have.

'To say that the only miracles that count are only those seen by thousands would do a huge injustice to the countless times miracles happen 'under the radar'. With Wendy, these are the miracles she must have, in order to survive – spiritually or otherwise.

'In God's sovereignty, He has brought her back from times when her body was so close to death and ready to give up and stop trying. But in each of those moments our miraculous God met with a faith-filled Wendy who had to trust Him just a little bit longer. She has always fought her way back knowing He just wasn't finished with her here yet.'

The reporter thought for a moment, then asked, 'What would you say then, to those hundreds of people who go to the stadiums, stand in line for hours hoping for a miracle?' The man had just spent a great deal of time writing and gathering information from those exact kinds of people. People who had just 'known' that they had to get to that stadium in order for them to get their 'touch' from God.

'Well, first we would say go. Go in faith believing. If God is telling them to go, who are we to say that God doesn't want to create a divine appointment for them at that stadium or at that service? On the flip side of that, however, is that the Bible also says that our God is no respecter of persons, which means that God can heal whenever and however and using whoever He wants to. He is sovereign. His ways, higher than ours.

'What I truly believe is that the same God, who is at that stadium, is also in the hospital sick room. He's the same God at the prayer ministry line at the altar of my church, as He is in my bedroom when I call on Him in the middle of the night. That gift of healing, those miracles, when God wills them to happen to show His power, He can and will use any willing vessel whose heart is after Him first.'

Wendy's dad looked earnestly into the reporter's eyes. 'Many years ago, there was a great healer who travelled around the world. This would have been the early 70's. Kathryn Kuhlman. Have you heard of her?'

The reporter nodded, as her name popped up in his research for faith healing for the previous articles he had written. 'Yes, she was quite powerful, from what I've read', he answered.

'Yes, she was. Well, Wendy's mother and I took Wendy when she was young, around five years old, I'd say. Our church had taken a busload of people to see her in Philadelphia. In those days, Wendy was so small I could carry her around everywhere in my arms.

'When we got to the stadium, there were hundreds of people, all waiting for their miracle. We stood in line and eventually got to head into the stadium. Wendy's mom went to the washroom, which was downstairs from where the service was being held.

'While I was standing there, holding Wendy in my arms, I felt something stir in my heart. It was like God was speaking right to me, asking me why I was there. As I looked at this little girl in my arms, I realized that she was okay. God was in control and that nothing about her needed to change. God changed me though. When her mom came back from the washroom, she told me that she felt God was saying that Wendy did not need to be here. That God would heal her in His time, not in ours. Both of us had had the same thought, at the same time, two different places in the building.

'Don't misunderstand me though. There was healing that happened that night. People who rode the bus with us from our church, they got a release from their physical pain, in their backs, and other issues. I really believe that Wendy's mom and I, both of our hearts got healed that night. God knew that we would need that kind of touch from Him to get Wendy through the next 46 years.'

Wendy's mom picked it up. 'As a parent, when you have just given birth, and then are taken to the nursery to be shown your child, you have every hope and dream for her. When the doctor says, there is your daughter in the incubator. She has brain damage, she's convulsing and probably won't live through the night, the expectations change in an instant. We prayed, it was all we could do really, and she lived through the night. That was our first miracle. And she's been living through every night for 46 years, more miracles.

'When, as a parent, you are told your child will never have any control over her muscular system, and you see that the doctors were right about that, she doesn't; again, expectations are very low. However, in a body that has no control over spasming muscles, Wendy was able to eventually learn how to chew food and swallow liquids from a cup without choking herself to death. Another miracle.

'As you are walking out of the hospital, not sure how to make it through to the next day, but you've got this little bundle in your arms, it becomes pretty clear, pretty fast that you had better trust in something more powerful than you.

'There were so many things that we were told that Wendy could not do. She has defied quite a few of them. To us, those are miracles.

'Communicating, for someone like Wendy, is nothing short of miraculous. Can you imagine someone with no voice and no ability to get their point across, finally learning a picture language and telling us she is thirsty for the first time? In school, Wendy learned the Bliss language. It is a picture language used by non-verbal people and Wendy learned how to use it every day.

'One of her teachers, early on, discovered that we could use her eyes to obtain yes and no answers, and from there, her symbol board was created. We tried head pointers in vain, finger pointing was out of the question; only her eyes worked consistently for her.

'It was another one of those every day miracles that gets overlooked in its importance because it's not the 'big' one. For us, it was huge. Opening up a communication system for her was vital. The fact that not only could she understand it, she learned to use it well, all this from a brain they said would not be able to understand anything.

'She still travels with a symbol board and it's always a relief for her that she has it when she's having trouble getting a point across.

'In the more recent years, perhaps the last 15 or so, her current method of communication is a voice output device. It is programmed with words and phrases and Wendy has worked hard to try and use this device as a voice. The beauty of her 'voice box' is that when it is attached to her chair, conversations with Wendy can be initiated by her.

The first time Wendy told us she loved us, using the voice box, in an actual voice, we cried. Can you imagine how that must have felt for her, after all the years not being able to hear the words she was trying to say, but now a voice is saying her thoughts out loud. It was incredible really.

'You see sir? What your readers need to understand is that there is a different perspective here on Wendy and her miracles. Once we walked out of that stadium, we knew that God had our backs. Our job was to love Wendy exactly as she was, exactly how He loved her, and create a space for her that let her be herself. That's what we have tried to do, that is what we still try to do. God would do the rest in His timing, and He has.'

'Well', the man said quietly.

CHAPTER SIX

Everyone was quiet at the table for a few moments, sipping the remnants of coffee, cleaning off plates with the last crusts of pie each of them had ordered for dessert.

The man looked at the mother and father sitting in front of him with renewed respect. He felt that they had earned the right to speak as frankly as they had spoken with him today. He felt nothing but love from them in their discussion of their daughter and it was humbling.

'There is one other thing you should know' the mother was adding quietly. 'Wendy has never given up the hope that God will heal her. She prays for that regularly. She brings her requests, such as her very painful back, issues at the house, prayer requests for others she has heard about - she brings those issues to prayer meetings and Sunday church believing that God cares about it all. Above all else though, she has never given up believing that God can heal her, in His time, and for His glory.'

The reporter knew what his next step needed to be. He felt that this time, when he visited Wendy, he was at least able to give her the respect that she deserved. She was peaceful to be around, he had felt that at his first visit, but it would be much more productive now that he understood where she came from.

"I'm sorry that I need to end this right now. I have a flight to catch so I must get a start to the airport. You have given me much to think about between now and when I visit with Wendy again. It is important that I go back and see her and speak with her, asking her some questions myself.'

The reporter didn't seem all that much in a hurry to leave, even though he was on a schedule. He wanted to hear more. He wanted to know this person; how could she carry so much heaviness and burden inside, and yet still manage to produce such peace around her?

'If you let us know when you want to stop by, we can definitely meet you there and help facilitate some discussion, if you like', Wendy's father offered.

'I will definitely be taking you up on that one. I'd really love to meet the Wendy that I've been introduced to today, give her and I another chance to get better acquainted.'

At that, the reporter touched the recording button on his phone, turning the device off, and went to the cash register to pay the bill. He signed for it to be charged to his room and then turned to Wendy's parents who were gathering themselves together to leave the restaurant.

'Thank you so much again. This truly has been such a pleasure. Thank you for taking the time to help me understand.' The man was genuine in his gratitude.

Wendy's father shook his hand. 'Anytime you need a question answered, we're here and happy to do that. Thank you for trying to understand her. We think she's pretty special.'

Wendy's mother leaned in to give the reporter a hug goodbye. 'Let us know when you want to meet at her house and we'll be there. Safe travels to you.'

CHAPTER SEVEN

It was a week after he had met Wendy's parents. He had flown to handle his commitments and come back. He had decided he wanted to see Wendy on his own. See if he could manage to understand her and communicate without her parents around.

He didn't call ahead or make an appointment at the house. He wanted to drop in and catch her just how she was every day. He hadn't been able to stop thinking about the interview he'd had with her parents. He didn't need much to complete his article, but he needed just something from Wendy herself. Something from her perspective.

He pulled into the driveway of a pleasant looking house. The last time he was here, he had second guessed himself wondering if he had the right address. The house didn't look like a home for disabled adults. It looked like a regular house on a regular street in a regular neighborhood. Quite comfortable, in fact.

Knocking on the door, he was greeted with a smile and a welcome. 'Can I help you?' a pleasant young woman asked from behind the door.

'I would like to spend a few minutes with Wendy, if I may. I didn't call ahead, I'm sorry for the lack of notice, but I was wondering if I could chat with her for a minute,' the man said, hoping luck was on his side.

'Oh I'm sorry. Wendy is out for the day. She has regular programs scheduled. Can I help you with something?'

He was disappointed. His deadline hadn't allowed him much flexibility to wait for her. 'I'm a reporter, doing a story on Wendy. I have been here before __' he started.

'Oh,' the woman interrupted, 'I think there is a package here for you. Wendy spent some time putting it together, with some help, that is. Just a second.'

He waited just inside the doorway as the woman went down the hall to Wendy's room. She came back just moments later with a large manila envelope, it had his name on it and he noticed instructions for it to be given to him if he ever came to the door.

'Did she know I was coming?' he asked.

'I'm not sure, but I have a feeling she knew your conversation wasn't done yet. I think she felt she needed to add something to what you went away with last time. I know she worked hard on these for you and one of our staff helped her print them and put them together.'

'Well thank you very much. I won't take up any more of your time,' the man said.

He walked back to his car in the driveway. He got in the car and sat behind the wheel, gathering his thoughts before he opened the envelope Wendy left for him.

He pulled out a pile of papers, clipped together with a paperclip. Leafing through them, just at a quick glance, he noticed they were poems, all with the name Wendy at the bottom. Each one was on a separate sheet, as if they were ready for submission for publication. 'She wrote these poems, and then left them for me?' he thought to himself.

He put the stack of papers back in the envelope, turned on his car and backed out of the driveway. 'This will be an interesting read', he said out loud, to no one in particular. He wanted to find somewhere quiet where he could read them with no disruption.

When he finally found a parking lot to turn into, near a park, he shut off his car, his cell phone, his tablet and his blue tooth. He reached into the envelope once again and pulled out the clipped stack.

He read each poem slowly. Then he read them all again equally slowly to allow the words on the page to truly sink in.

Coming away from the interview with Wendy's parents had left the seasoned reporter humbled and wanting to meet with Wendy again to fill in some blanks about how she herself felt.

Upon reading her poetry, the man knew exactly how she felt. The words stunned him and pulled him in. He had what he needed for his article, exactly the personal side he was looking for, presented by Wendy herself.

He didn't require further interviews with her to finish the story, but he thought he just might go back at some point and visit with her again. He felt like he was missing something in his life and he wondered if meeting with Wendy and her parents might give him a clue how to find the peace that she had.

One thing was for certain, he felt that assignment or not, his life was fuller for having intersected with Wendy, on any level.

The

Wendy

Poems

Control

There is a degree of
Panic
In my every day
Panic and
Blind trust

When I was young
Someone was
Always there
Who understood
Who saw my face
And figured out my need
Someone protected me
Someone made me laugh
Someone knew when I cried
When I was young
Someone
Carried me

I am a woman now
I know fear
Fear of being left alone
Fear of being misunderstood or ignored
Fear of being lost

Sometimes I wonder
About drivers
And caregivers
And people

I keep working hard
To control my fear
And trust that belts on busses are secure

I keep working hard
To control my panic
When going
Alone
Somewhere new

I keep working very hard
To control my need for control

Even when I want to
I cannot have a driver
Triple check
Locking mechanisms on belts in vans
No matter how badly I want them to
I cannot force people
To use
A blissboard to try and understand me
Even when things make me crazy
I cannot cry out
Every time
I panic
About all the things
I cannot control

I am a woman now

What I know to be true
What brings peace
To override my fear
Is that those
'Someone's'
Those special 'someone's'
Are still here in my life
Watching and
Listening and
Carrying me

Those 'Someone's'
Family and friends and staff
Take my fear
And cradle me
Overcoming
My fear and
My need to control
With love
And safety
And laughter
And music

And love.

.....perfect love casts out all fear.....

....Wendy

Heaven

Heaven is my home
Heaven is my hope
He is there
Waiting for me

My home is being prepared
For me

For me

Not for a chair
Or a lift
Or a hospital bed
But for me
Me and my new body

He is there
Waiting for me
To walk with me
And talk with me
Using my new legs
Using my new voice

He is there
And He will tell me
You have cried enough
There are no tears here
He will tell me
That I don't have to sit
That I can stand
With my new body
I have sat long enough

Heaven is my home
It is where I belong
He will let me sing
With the angels
With my new voice
He will let me dance
With loved ones
With my new legs
He will let me
Touch and hold everything
With my new arms

Heaven is my home
He is my hope
Struggle and
Pain and
Tears
Are only for a time

Because
Heaven is my home.

....Wendy

His Voice

Someone asked me once
'Does God talk to you?'
I said no
I hear no voices in the night
No audible sound
Revealing something new

What He does
Is whisper
Sweetness to me
In my heart
What He does
Is hum
Quietly into the
Marrow of my bones

It's not what I hear
Outside myself
That changes me
It's what happens
Where nobody sees
On the inside

I would feel
So unworthy
If I heard God speak
Directly, out loud to me
Because I
Cannot reply

I am
Beyond
Myself
Excited that
After all this time

The very first time I hear
......His Voice
Is the very first time
........He hears mine

....Wendy

The Race

They all talk about a
Race to be run
Run the race, they say
Fight the good fight, they go on

I cannot run
I cannot fight
What happens to me?
Am I sidelined?
I can't even get TO the race
How do I run it?

Lots of things they talk about
Demand a
Physical response
Demand a
Gesture or a movement or a fight
To prove worthiness

These things escape me
Every day feels like
The good fight
It's all I can do to
Pray and praise and carry on

The truth is
We all have
A race to run
Yours just looks different
Than mine

My heart is on
This journey
Just like yours

Fighting and trying

It looks
Different
But feels
The same
In our hearts

I know we are not alone

Just as He is
Running with you
He is pushing
Me and my chair

And we are all
In the race

....Wendy

I Am Easy

Lots of people
Are afraid
Afraid of big things
And small things
Afraid of things
Outside themselves
And sometimes
They fear
Something on the inside

I can see
When you look at me
And my chair
Sometimes
It scares you
Or
Makes you nervous
It's always been that way
From the time I was little
People were
Nervous and jittery
Around me

This makes me
Smile
Sometimes
Because I cannot
Leave this chair
I cannot
Pounce on you
I cannot
Hurt you

What is there to fear?

I am easy

You can approach me
And talk
As if I understand
Everything you say
As if I 'get'
Your jokes
As if I hear
When you pray over me

Because
What you really
Need to know

Is that I do
Understand it and 'get' it and hear you

And I will not hurt you

If you give me a chance
He will help us both
Figure each other out

Do not be afraid of me
I will not hurt you
I will listen to you
I will laugh with you

But I will not
Laugh
If your joke is not funny

....Wendy

Love

Love changes everything
What does love look like?

Love is
    My Grandma
    Whose prayer wheel never stopped turning
    And who is first in line in heaven waiting for me
Love is
    My sisters
    Who treat me like I'm normal
    But who love me like I'm special
Love is
    My parents
    Looking out for me
    Every single day
    Of my whole entire life
Love is
    My family
    With new loving additions
    And my aunts and uncles
    And niece and nephews
    And cousins
    Because they are the loud, fun cushion
    That surrounds me and reminds me
    I am a part of a crazy, wild, amazing family
Love is
    Friends who need wheels too
    Because we understand each other
Love is
    Angels disguised as special teachers and therapists
    Who saw more in me
    With their heart
    Than with their eyes

Love is
        Church ladies who pray
        Because prayer changes things
Love is
        Pastors
        Who have seen more in me
        With their spirit
        Than with their eyes
Love is
        Doctors and nurses
        Because God has used them
        To create miracles for me
Love is
        Angels disguised as staff
        Who smile and look me in the eye
        As they help me be
        The best version of me
        Every single day
Love is
        Churches
        Who let me
        Be myself and enter into worship
        As loudly and as clumsily
        As I sometimes do
Love is
        My very special friends who don't need wheels
        Because they understand
        That I hear them
        And I need them
        Just as much
        As they need me

              Love is powerful
               Love is moving
              Love is amazing

My life is full to overflowing
With love
Love that is powerful
And moving
And amazing

The miracle of my world
Is how much love actually surrounds me
Every single day

....Wendy

Broken

When I speak, I waste no words
When I pray, I have no perfection
I am broken
My God deserves better

My arms won't rise in worship
My legs won't stand to revere Him
My voice cannot utter one syllable – even of halting praise
I am broken
I am not stupid or blind or deaf
I am not unfeeling
I am not careless with my emotions
I see and hear and feel
Everything

I am a woman
Simply
A broken woman

In days past
The pain was not constant
And blinding
In days past
My body's betrayal
Was quick and jerky and spasmodic

Today
My body wars with my soul
Today
The pain screams to drown Him out
Today
My soft, fleshy heart is torn into a
Million pained pieces

In days past
My hope was in
Tomorrows
Down the road
That glorious
Someday

Today
As my angels
Have gone before me
The fragile hope is
Today
Release must be
Today

For I am broken

My body betrays me
Every waking minute

My hope is
Him

Him – who has loved me
Him – who has seen me
Him – who has carried me

Him – who cares not about voices
Him – who cares very little about flailing arms and legs
Him – who cares a great deal about my hope

I cannot speak – therefore I waste no words
My prayers are little more than noises
But my heart ...my heart is Him

He is the One
Who has been broken too
He is the One
Whose arms were nailed and could not lift in praise
He is the One
Whose legs were nailed so He could not rise in reverence
He is the One
Who lost His voice when He was broken on a cross

I am broken
But He was broken too

I will continue today
To hope
I will continue today
To love

Love Him
Who loves me right back

Me and my brokenness

....Wendy

Constant Pain

When pain is your visitor
Every day
You go to bed
Praying tomorrow
Will be different

When pain is your visitor
Every day
You pray that
You will wake up
And it will not hurt to breathe

When pain is your visitor
Every day
You pray in the morning
That your day won't be completely steam-rollered
By how bad everything hurts

When pain is your visitor
Every day
It feels like everything you do
Is taken over
By its endless torture

When pain is your visitor
Every day
It takes over
And makes you forget
Who actually lives in your heart

He has promised
He will rescue
He will heal

When pain is my visitor
Every day
It lies to me
Telling me
There is no hope

Sometimes I forget
That He has promised
That He will rescue
And that He will heal

When pain is my visitor
Every day
Sometimes
It's hard to remember
That pain will not win.

...Wendy

Worship

God created music right?
He made Elvis sing
Love Me Tender
Debby Boone sing
You Light Up My Life
And Don Moen sing
God Will Make a Way

These songs
Make me cry
I love music
It lifts me
Where I can't go
On my own

My sister sings
Like how I think an angel sings
It makes me cry too

Worship is my
Favourite
Because it wraps itself
Around the deepest parts
Both the good
And the bad
The singers sing
The words I cannot
Taking my praise up to Him

Sometimes
The worship
Brings His love
Right down to me
Where I sit

Worship
Is constantly
Moving
Lifting Him up
Then at the same time
Wrapping around
All of us

Sometimes when the
Worship
Is loud enough
I join in with
My faltering, loud cry
I sometimes
Am overwhelmed
In worship
It moves me so

I'm so thankful
He accepts my worship

I'm so thankful
He created music

....Wendy

The Special Ones

Every once in a while
God gives me one special person
Who sees past the chair
Who sees past the parts of me
That don't work

Every once in a while
Someone comes along
Who makes me forget
For a few minutes
About how hard it is
To communicate
They just seem to know

They make me feel
That I don't even have to try
To get them to understand
They make me feel
That I can trust them
With the stuff inside me that hurts

Every once in a while
A rose blooms in the desert
A comet streaks across the sky
And every once in a while
Someone very special
Comes along and makes me feel

Beautiful and
Normal and
Complete

...Wendy

Faith

Do I believe Him?
Yes
Every single time
In every way

Do I trust Him?
Yes
With everything
My heart holds dear

Do I love Him?
Always
Forever
For eternity

What I have been taught
And how I've grown
To live
Is that this is the definition of
Faith

Faith is
Believing
With your heart
What your eyes and your head
Tell you
Is impossible

Belief
Trust
Love
Are all the definitions of
My life with God

The pain
And frustration
And difficulty
Are strong
And hard
And tiring

But even in those times

Do I still believe Him?
Yes
Every time
And in every way

Do I still trust Him?
Yes
With everything
My mind and heart and strength
Can muster

Do I still love Him?
Yes – always
A thousand times – yes
Forever
And for
Eternity

This is my healing faith

.....Wendy

2 Corinthians 4:18

While we look not at the things which are seen, but at the things which are not seen: for the things which are seen are temporal; but the things which are not seen are eternal.